Greater Than a Tourist Book
Series
Reviews from Readers

I think the series is wonderful and beneficial for tourists to get information before visiting the city.

-Seckin Zumbul, Izmir Turkey

I am a world traveler who has read many trip guides but this one really made a difference for me. I would call it a heartfelt creation of a local guide expert instead of just a guide.

-Susy, Isla Holbox, Mexico

New to the area like me, this is a must have!

-Joe, Bloomington, USA

This is a good series that gets down to it when looking for things to do at your destination without having to read a novel for just a few ideas.

-Rachel, Monterey, USA

Good information to have to plan my trip to this destination.

-Pennie Farrell, Mexico

Great ideas for a port day.

-Mary Martin USA

Aptly titled, you won't just be a tourist after reading this book. You'll be greater than a tourist!

-Alan Warner, Grand Rapids, USA

Even though I only have three days to spend in San Miguel in an upcoming visit, I will use the author's suggestions to guide some of my time there. An easy read - with chapters named to guide me in directions I want to go.

-Robert Catapano, USA

Great insights from a local perspective! Useful information and a very good value!

-Sarah, USA

This series provides an in-depth experience through the eyes of a local. Reading these series will help you to travel the city in with confidence and it'll make your journey a unique one.

-Andrew Teoh, Ipoh, Malaysia

GREATER THAN A TOURIST- OHIO USA

50 Travel Tips from a Local

Crystal Wolcott

Cover designed by: Ivana Stamenkovic
Cover Image: https://pixabay.com/en/columbus-ohio-city-urban-buildings-1936114/

CZYK Publishing Since 2011.

Greater Than a Tourist
Visit our website at www.GreaterThanaTourist.com

Lock Haven, PA
ISBN: 9781724106995

>TOURIST

50 TRAVEL TIPS FROM A LOCAL

BOOK DESCRIPTION

Are you excited about planning your next trip?

Do you want to try something new?

Would you like some guidance from a local?

If you answered yes to any of these questions, then this Greater Than a Tourist book is for you.

Greater Than a Tourist- Ohio USA gives you the inside scoop on Ohio. Most travel books tell you how to travel like a tourist. Although there is nothing wrong with that, as part of the Greater Than a Tourist series, this book will give you travel tips from someone who has lived at your next travel destination.

In these pages, you will discover advice that will help you throughout your stay. This book will not tell you exact addresses or store hours but instead will give you excitement and knowledge from a local that you may not find in other smaller print travel books.

Travel like a local. Slow down, stay in one place, and get to know the people and the culture. By the time you finish this book, you will be eager and prepared to travel to your next destination.

TABLE OF CONTENTS

DEDICATION

To my family, who is always there for me. To my friends who support me no matter what. To my teachers, who have shaped me. To my cats, who have cuddled me.

-This is for you.

ABOUT THE AUTHOR

Traveling since 2011, Crystal Wolcott is a 24-year-old writer and blogger currently based in the US. What began as a vacation with her big sister, has become a lifelong passion, and career. So far her travels have taken her to three continents and more than 20 countries. Growing up in Ohio, she always dreamed of traveling the world and is currently making that dream a reality. She supports herself with freelance writing and blogging while on the road. She is a queer plus-sized woman, who is striving to make the world a more accepting place. An activist and a leader, Crystal is a natural force ready to make her mark on the world. BargainNomad.com

HOW TO USE THIS BOOK

The Greater Than a Tourist book series was written by someone who has lived in an area for over three months. The goal of this book is to help travelers either dream or experience different locations by providing opinions from a local. The author has made suggestions based on their own experiences. Please do your own research before traveling to the area in case the suggested places are unavailable.

FROM THE PUBLISHER

Traveling can be one of the most important parts of a person's life. The anticipation and memories that you have are some of the best. As a publisher of the Greater Than a Tourist book series, as well as the popular 50 Things to Know book series, we strive to help you learn about new places, spark your imagination, and inspire you. Wherever you are and whatever you do I wish you safe, fun, and inspiring travel.

Lisa Rusczyk Ed. D.
CZYK Publishing

OUR STORY

Traveling is a passion of the "Greater than a Tourist" series creator. Lisa studied abroad in college, and for their honeymoon Lisa and her husband toured Europe. During her travels to Malta, an older man tried to give her some advice based on his own experience living on the island since he was a young boy. She was not sure if she should talk to the stranger but was interested in his advice. When traveling to some places she was wary to talk to locals because she was afraid that they weren't being genuine. Through her travels, Lisa learned how much locals had to share with tourists. Lisa created the "Greater Than a Tourist" book series to help connect people with locals. A topic that locals are very passionate about sharing.

WELCOME TO
> TOURIST

INTRODUCTION

Ohio is the state everyone knows of, yet so few know well. This land displays rolling hills and extensive planes, of lush green vegetation and blue, blue waters. It is truly the heartland of America. Here you can discover ancient monuments and witness cutting-edge science. Here you can see people whose way of life hasn't changed in a millennia or visit the bustling centers of some of America's greatest cities. Ohio is diverse, with people coming from all over the world to call it home. From the German populations who have been here over a century to the new Ghanaian population, it's easy to learn about a different culture or to hear a foreign tongue on the breeze.

For me it is more than that; for me it is home. Ohio is where I come to feel at peace, the place where I know I'll be accepted and welcomed with open arms. This is where I feel community. The people here are welcoming. You can't walk into a shop without hearing a lighthearted "Hello!" float your way. The locals work hard for what they have, growing crops that support a good chunk of American agriculture. When they're not working they know how to have a good time: whether playing at a state of the art theme park or vacationing on the Lake Erie shore. Ohioans know how to have a good time.

So join us. Spend some time relaxing and getting to know the good ol' folks of Ohio. Visit one of our many festivals, parks, gardens, or museums, and sit back for the best trip of your life.

1. RELAX ON THE SHORES OF LAKE ERIE

Lake Erie is the only great lake in Ohio; in fact, it's the only natural lake in Ohio. All other lakes are man-made, most due to damming. Like her sisters, Lake Erie was carved out of the earth by melting glaciers about 14,000 years ago near the end of the Great Ice Age. This can be seen in the glacial grooves on Kelleys Island. The lake gets its name from the original inhabitants of the areas, the Erie Native American tribe. Eventually, they were conquered by the Iroquois and the land would eventually wind up in the Iroquois Confederacy, along with people of the Ottawa, Wyandot, and Mingo tribes.

Europeans arrived on the scene in 1669 with French trader and explorer Louis Jolliet in 1669. The lake would later become infamous during the war of 1812 in the Battle of Lake Erie, where Oliver Hazard Perry defeated the British in a tempestuous water battle. The area's rich history is easy to explore with museums and historical sites throughout the area.

Today Lake Erie is a vacation region, the shoreline between Toledo and Cleveland boasts beautiful sand and rock beaches. Near Cleveland, some of the most popular beaches are Huntington

Beach in Bay Village, Edgewater Beach near downtown, and Headlands State Park, near Mentor. It is home to some of the largest commercial freshwater fisheries in the country.

Hop a ferry from the mainland and explore Put-in-Bay on South Bass Island, Kelleys Island or Middle Bass. Fishing for sport is also a popular way to spend one's time while visiting Lake Erie so look for walk-on fishing charter in the harbor when you visit. Any recreation equipment like kayaks, canoes, or paddle boards can be rented there, so it's easy to get out and explore. Visit again in the spring for the songbird migration or in the winter to try your hand at ice fishing.

2. YOU CAN VISIT ANYTIME

Ohio is a great place to visit year round. In the spring our public gardens, such as Inniswood Metro Gardens, Dawes Arboretum, or Kingswood Center are full of blooms and offer the perfect sunny afternoon activity. Amusement parks like Cedar Point, Kings Island, and Zoombezi Bay and festivals such as the Strawberry Festival, the Ice Cream

Festival and the Dublin Irish Festival fill the summer with adventure and memories.

Autumn brings incredible experiences. We celebrate the foliage at places like Mohican State Park, and everything pumpkin at the Circleville Pumpkin Show. Winter is magical with snow-covered trees, and a chance to celebrate the season at the Columbus Zoo WildLights shows. Ohio has something fun going on at all times of the year. To find out what will be happening during your visit, head over to Ohio.org and check out the calendar of events. My favorite season in Ohio will always be the autumn.

3. EXPLORE CINCINNATI

Sitting at the midpoint of the Ohio River is the glistening city of Cincinnati. It covers the southwestern corner of Ohio, and its greater metropolitan area sprawls into Northern Kentucky and southeastern Indiana. Originally named "Losantiville" by one of the first settlers to the area, John Filson, Cincinnati was also the site of Fort Washington, giving the area protection to grow into the modern metropolis it is now. Renamed Cincinnati in 1790 after the Society of Cincinnati, an organization of Revolutionary War officers, the town would continue to develop into a city with a thriving culture all its own.

Cincinnati's modern downtown is compact and easy to navigate. With major league sports and four-star restaurants calling the areas home, it's the perfect place for an outing. Unfortunately, Cincinnati has had some difficulty getting their public transportation system up to snuff, with a planned subway in the 1900s falling to the wayside during the Great Depression. (Tours of the abandoned tunnels are available online.) Today the city is proud of its new electric streetcar system. The streetcar is a 3.6-mile loop connecting important communities in the city's urban center. Running every day of the year with over 2000 passengers a day, this loop is the start of what the city hopes will be a sprawling system connecting the whole city together.

4. GO SPELUNKING IN SEARCH OF THE "CRYSTAL KING."

The Ohio Caverns in Dover, Ohio were discovered in 1897 by a farmhand, Robert Noffsinger. He noticed a sinkhole that had been filled with water had suddenly emptied overnight. Under the farmlands of western Ohio, he discovered an underground river flowing through multiple caverns and depositing silt and mud in its wake. Soon after its discovery tourist and thieves vandalized the caverns, stealing crystals and writing their names on the walls.

Allen and Ira Smith purchased the land and began the process of cleaning up the mud and were able to lengthen the traversable parts of the cavern from a quarter-mile to over two miles. Today all the four chambers are available to be toured, called Fantasyland," "The Big Room," "The Jewel Room," and "Palace of the Gods." The showstopper is The Crystal King," a solid white stalactite almost five feet long and over 200,000 years old.

5. LOOK FOR FESTIVALS YEAR ROUND

Ohio has a lot of festivals. In fact, there are more than 1300 every year. The Dublin Irish Festival is the largest Irish festival outside of Ireland. It usually boasts more than 100,000 attendees and takes place the first weekend of August. The Ohio Renaissance Festival takes place over nine weekends starting with Labor Day Weekend. Located in Waynesville it has everything over 150 arts and craftsman shops as well as 12 stages. Just outside of Utica is the memorial day Ice Cream Festival at the Velvet Ice Cream factory. Check out the vendor's booths and the ice cream eating contest. For strawberry lovers check out the Troy Strawberry Festival the first weekend of June. Here you will find strawberry everything from kebabs to cheesecake. Looking for something a little more out of the ordinary? Try the Twins Day festival or the Duck Tape Festival. Twinsburg is the home to the Twins Day Festival, every first weekend of August, twins descend on the town dressed to fit the theme of the year. On Father's Day weekend head to Avon for the Heritage Duct Tape Festival, where you can check out, buy or even make amazing duct tape creations.

6. COLUMBUS'S GERMAN VILLAGE

German Village is an old-world neighborhood with book and coffee shops, restaurants and bars. In 1865, one-third of Columbus's population was German or of German descent. Many German heroes of the revolutionary war had settled in the area just south of downtown, renaming the area German Village. Up until World War I, most public schools taught German to its pupils. When strong anti-German ideals came to the area textbooks were burned and local German sites were renamed to reflect more Anglican heritage.

Ironically this neighborhood would produce Ohio's most well-known war hero, Captain Eddie Rickenbacker, one of America's best fighter pilots in WWI. With German signs all around it's a great place to go to get a taste of early German life in America. From beautiful houses to adorable bookstores you can easily spend an afternoon exploring and eating in German Village. The area has also been a place where many oppressed people have taken refuge over the years. Today it is known as Columbus's "gayborhood," where many older LGBTQ residents live. German Village is a testament to that heritage of coming together across enemy lines.

7. EXPLORE LOCAL HISTORY IN FRIENDLY NEWARK

Newark, a quintessential town in central Ohio, has a lot to offer. The Downtown National Historic Register District is a directory of beautiful houses and buildings in downtown Newark that are chock full of history. The National Heisey Glass Museum is perfect for young and old lovers of the art of glassmaking. For the brave of heart, the Licking County Historic Jail offers ghost hunts open to the public. For some art take in the Midland theatre or the Newark-Granville Symphony Orchestra.

Take some time off in nature in visit the Blackhand Gorge State Nature Preserve, a park with easy to challenging trails getting its name from the hand-shaped Native American petroglyph on a cliff face on the north side of the river. The area is full of mementos from the time before the colonizers. Newark Earthworks, a recreation of original native mounds sits in the center of town, with bits of the original earthworks visible throughout town. Just outside of town on state route 37 is the Great Serpent Mound, an original mount built by Fort Ancient culture around 1070 BCE with earlier works dating back to 300 BCE, thought to be of Adena construction. There are several Native American sites in the area to check out.

8. SET SAIL TO KELLEYS ISLAND

In the western basin of Lake Erie lies the beautiful Kelleys Island. Easily reachable from Cleveland, Toledo, and Sandusky, Kelleys Island is the perfect weekend getaway from a metropolitan heavy tour. The island has miniature golf, available at Caddyshack Square, plenty of boats, bikes, and golf carts to rent. When you tire of physical activities the island has over a half-dozen shops, offering souvenirs, T-shirts and items for the home.

Kelleys Island State Park, covering almost 700 acres, with sandy beaches and over six miles of hiking trails, truly is a gem in the crown of Kelleys Island. Take a walk along the North Pond State Nature Preserve mile-long boardwalk, for beautiful land and water vistas.

A highlight of the island is the glacial grooves which were carved into the limestone almost 20,000 years ago by ice-flows as they drifted south. The 400 foot-long groves contain marine fossils, thought to be hundreds of millions of years old. They are thought to be the largest grooves in the world that are accessible to be studied.

Local artist Charles Herndon works with materials, and inspiration found right on Kelleys Island. His glass, wood, stone, and metal artworks are showcased in a museum on the island, where he also has pieces for sale.

The rest of the island has a lot to offer as well. It's sleepier than it's popular neighbor Put-in-Bay, which is why it's so easy to feel like a local here. Have dinner at a local restaurant like The Casino, which no longer offers gambling, but does offer some of the best drinks on the island. Settle down in one of the many shoreline restaurants to watch the boats coming in and the sun dipping below Lake Erie.

9. BUY SOME GROCERIES

In Ohio, there are some really great grocery stores. Like most of the nation, there are Targets and Walmarts everywhere, but the stores that are local to the region have a better selection of local foods. Kroger is the regional grocery store chain, it has everything you could want from organic tofu to freshly baked bread. Aldi, the American version of the German original, is great for those who are a bit more budget conscious.

Local markets are a great way to go as well, check out North Market in Columbus, Findlay Market in Cincinnati, and 2nd Street Market in Dayton. Be sure to look for local markets in every town as most large towns have great local markets as well as International ones. In the summer most towns have a local farmers market on the weekends that can be looked up on the internet.

Ohio is very picnic friendly. Most parks, monuments, and sites you'll visit will definitely have an area to picnic. If you're staying somewhere with a kitchen even better! You can experiment with local ingredients to try making local recipes.

10. VISIT THE OUT OF COMMISSION PRISON MADE FAMOUS BY THE SHAWSHANK REDEMPTION.

The Ohio State Reformatory in Mansfield, Ohio was made famous by the film The Shawshank Redemption, but its true nature is even more disturbing. Used for all of the exterior shots and a few interior ones for the 1994 movie, the Ohio State Reformatory was built between 1886 and 1910 but has been closed since December 1990. The exterior is impressively large with what is often described as Germanic castle architecture. Much of the prison has been demolished, however, the East Cell Block remains, and is actually the largest free-standing steel cell block in the entire world rising six tiers above the ground floor.

Many believe the place to be haunted, with over 200 deaths in and around the prison while it was still in operation, including a few guards who were killed during various escape attempts. The most popular spirit hotspots include the two chapels, the infirmary, the solitary confinement section, and the warden's office

11. DON'T FORGET ESSENTIALS

The weather in Ohio can change quickly it can be sunny one minute and snowing the next. Constantly check the weather to know what to expect every day. Depending on when you are visiting, you need to bring season appropriate items. In the summer it is very important to bring bug spray and sunscreen. The winters can be cold, make sure you have gloves and warm shoes. Any time of year you'll want an umbrella, raincoat, rain boots or whatever raingear you usually require. If you forget anything important, its possible to buy it here. Even ethnic foods and specialty items have a shop you can find easily enough.

12. TAR HOLLOW

Tar Hollow State Park twist through over 600 acres of forest and roadways. Covering deep ravines and dense woodlands with scattered shortleaf and pitch pines adorning the ridges. These trees used to be a source of pine tar for early settlers, which is where the valley gets its name from. In the spring dogwoods, redbuds and a variety of wildflowers color the hillsides, turning leafy green in the summer, and slowly dipping into the fantastic autumn foliage. The park boasts seventeen miles of paved forest roads and fourteen miles of gravel forest roads, making it the perfect place for a scenic drive.

13. AIRPORT INTEL

Cincinnati/Northern Kentucky International Airport (CVG) is a major Delta hub, many transcontinental trips are routed through for a total of almost 8 Million passengers every year. It offers direct connections to major easy cost cities including Atlanta, Orlando, Los Angeles, and New York. While convenient and easily accessible from the city center, this airport doesn't offer many amenities, making your visit quick but a little basic.

The Columbus Metropolitan Hub (CMH) or the John Glenn International Airport in Columbus Ohio is a Southwest hub and is actually a great airport for flying in and out of Ohio. Though it may be small it has everything you need from direct International connections to a Starbucks in every terminal. It's small enough that security is never too difficult to get through with each terminal having its own security checkpoint, ensuring the process is faster for everyone.

Cleveland Hopkins International Airport (CLE), the largest in Ohio, is often considered the gateway to the Midwest for international visitors. At the same time, it is also a hub for low-cost carrier ExpressJet Airlines, offering connections to many

North American destinations. While already offering one of the smoothest out-of-airport transport systems in the world, they are always upgrading their facilities to better serve its over 9 million passengers each year.

14. HARRY ANDREWS' CHATEAU LAROCHE

Harry Andrews was a medieval enthusiast, who was a notary public by day. While he never married he is reported to have had relationships with both men and women. When he retired at age 55, he began construction on his 1/5th scale replica of a medieval castle in Loveland, Ohio. All the building work he completed on his own using over 2,600 sacks of cement, 54,000 five-gallon buckets of dirt, and 56,000 pail-fulls of stone. His design was impeccable, he even hid a secret room that wasn't found until it collapsed several years after his death.

Unfortunately, he only spent two weeks in his masterpiece and lifelong dream. In a freak accident, he set himself on fire while cooking dinner and died soon thereafter. It's a fun place to visit, learn about its history, and understand its construction. Be warned, the locals unsurprisingly claim its haunted by

Andrew's ghost. Maybe he gets to spend eternity watching people enjoy the castle he worked so hard to build.

15. NIGHT LIFE

Ohio has many options for when the sun goes down. Our large cities have lots of great bars and clubs. Check out the Euclid Tavern and Grog Shop in Cleveland or stop by Oddfellows Liquor Bar or the bars along High Street in Columbus. Also in Columbus is COSI after dark, a night for adults to drink and check out the science center at the same time. For clubbing head to Mt. Addams Pavilion in Cincinnati. Looking for something outside of the city? Look for local dive bars, they all have something different waiting for you inside. If you really want to get a taste for the local folk, checking out where they drink is a must.

Not a drinker? No worries, we got you covered too. Dee Felice Cafe is a great Jazz club in Cincinnati. Check out the stand-up scene by stopping by the Columbus Funny Bone, a well known local comedy club. Cleveland's famous House of Blues has great live music year round. If you are willing to do a little research beforehand, you can easily find tickets to theater and live music events as well.

16. MEANDER THROUGH NORTHEAST OHIO'S WINE COUNTRY

The state of Ohio has over 100 wineries many which exist right along Lake Erie. The area actually boasts more wineries per square mile than in any other region in Ohio. The sharp sea breezes and the breathtaking views of Lake Erie ensures that the vintners produce grapes and make wine amid some of the country's most scenic vistas.

Even though the region is considered a 'cool climate' growing district, families have been tending to their historic vineyards here for generations with new vineyards of Rieslings and chardonnays opening all the time. Ferrante Winery & Ristorante in Ashtabula County and Laurentia Vineyard in Lake County are local favorites. Here you can experience Ohio's unique, locally-produced wine up close and personal. The cost of Lake Erie marks an unofficial wine trail, all you need is a car and a love of wine.

17. HARTMAN'S ROCK GARDEN

Springfield, Ohio's rock garden contains over an estimated 20,000 stones, all handpicked, broken down to size, and place by H.G. "Ben" Hartman. Hartman's Garden was started in 1932 while doing a project in the yard lining a fish pond. Over the next several years of unemployment due to the Great Depression, he used his time to build a sprawling rock wonderland in his yard. Strickenly different from the surrounding houses, even Hartman's white picket fence is made of stone.

The Rock Garden has everything from original creations to replicas of famous buildings including Philadelphia's Independence Hall, a White House, a Mount Vernon, and a large castle with a drawbridge. Stone animals march into a stone Noah's Ark and George Washington waves from his porch.

The garden still stands today, decayed somewhat, with moss and bugs making homes in the various nooks and crannies. Hartman passed the property on to his son, and today his grandchildren are looking to hire someone to keep the garden and surrounding property up. Visit one man's creative outlet and see the beauty that rose from the depths of America's depression.

18. THE CUYAHOGA VALLEY NATIONAL PARK

Nestled between Cleveland and Akron, the Cuyahoga Valley National Park feels like you are years away from the bustle of city life. A journey of discovery waiting to happen, the park is a refuge for local flora and fauna and an important historical landmark. The Cuyahoga River meanders through a lush forest which gives way to rolling hills and eventually green farmland.

Stop in at the Canal Visitor Center for a brief history of the canal and valley, and sign up for anger-led tours and special events. Follow the Towpath Trail, take in the beauty of Tinkers Creek Gorge, and contemplate the Brandywine Falls. This little slice of nature is Ohio's favorite national park.

19. CELEBRATE THE REJUVENATION IN COLUMBUS

Columbus, the state capital of Ohio, is a tourist-free gem. The bustling metropolis of over 1 million with its many distinct and quaint neighborhoods, manages to feel like a small town everywhere you look. With a resident symphony, art museums, a world-famous zoo, botanical gardens, a conservatory, universities, great shopping, and fabulous dining and live music scene, it's a wonder Columbus remains tourist free

Columbus has a great Metroparks system, parks like the Scioto Mile give nature enthusiast a green space to relax and rejuvenate from the city. Blacklick Woods Metro Park, Columbus Rose Garden, and Inniswood Metro Gardens offer beauty and an afternoon surrounded by nature. Franklin Park Conservatory, modeled after the Glass Palace at the Columbian Exposition in Chicago, is just out of the downtown area and offers 28 acres of English gardens and rare flora, with four indoor plant habits adorned with handcrafted blown glass by Dale Chihuly. For cyclists, the Olentangy-Scioto Bikeway or along the 52-mile Dublin Bicycle Loop offer solid trails and great views with plenty of interesting places to stop along the way.

Kids love to visit COSI, the Center of Science and Industry, which now has a permanent Dinosaur Gallery, but it has plenty to offer to adults. A few times a month after hours it transforms into a themed night, such as murder mystery, the ticket includes dinner and access to all the regular exhibits, now with alcohol in hand. The newly opened LEGOLAND Discovery Center is just one of the many things Easton Town Center has to offer. With over 250 stores and services, this village of a shopping center is a great place to spend some time, and some money.

Columbus doesn't skimp on sports either. With minors, majors and collegiate sports areas across town, there is always something happening. Check out professional Soccer at the Columbus Crew SC, Columbus Blue Jackets play hockey at Nationwide Arena, and the Columbus Clippers an MLB AAA team, play baseball at Huntington Park. Ohio State University has in season sports ongoing throughout the year, with football being a local favorite.

20. VISIT THE SITE OF SOJOURNER TRUTH'S 'AIN'T I A WOMAN?' SPEECH

On May 29, 1851, Sojourner Truth delivered her iconic "Ain't I a Woman?" speech from the Old Stone Church on High Street in Akron, Ohio. Today you can visit the spot where she stood, and read or listen (as there are sometimes reenactments) to her famous word as they would have drifted over the Little Cuyahoga River. Her words have gone down in history as one of the most important feminist and abolitionist speeches.

21. SOAK UP CLEVELAND'S UNIQUE CULTURE

Cleveland has been used as a substitute for New York in several movies including the recent Avengers movie from 2012. Ohio is actually quite a popular place to film due to the tax incentives to film here. Many movies including Air Force One and Happy Gilmore were also filmed in Cleveland.

The West Side Market, a centerpiece of historic Cleveland, has been open and in operation for over 100 years. It's spacious interior boast over 100 local businesses selling everything from fresh meat and cheese to local handicrafts and fresh flowers. It has earned the moniker "Cleveland's Public Market," from the locals, and gives visitors a place to dive in and taste the local cuisine. Stock up for a picnic, or gather enough to take home for a buffet of fresh local specialties.

22. DAYTON, HEROES OF AVIATION

Dayton, Ohio must be an inspirational place to live, as many famous inventions that we use in our everyday lives come from this modest burg. It is the birthplace of aviation, and it was here that three very talented men Wilbur and Orville Wright and Paul Laurence Dunbar, (an under-credited African American) not only advanced humanity but gave hope to the American people that our great nation that if we dare to dream it, it can be done. Through trial and much, much error, they were able to change how we see and explore our world.

In Dayton, there are six important sites to take in as part of the history of aviation. These must-see sites start with the Wright Cycle Company building, and continue on through the Hoover Block, Huffman Prairie Flying Field, 1905 Wright Flyer III, Hawthorn Hill, and the Paul Laurence Dunbar State Memorial. This flight history trail is great for kids as well. Pick up a "Race to Dayton's Amazing Aviation Places" passport. Be sure to visit 7 of the 16 National Aviation Heritage Area (NAHA.org) sites have your passport stamped to get a "Wilbear Wright Aviator Teddy Bear!"

Swing by the National Museum of the United States Air Force to see an impressive collection of US Air Force planes and something special, the 1952 Avrocar. The Avrocar is a man-made flying saucer developed by the United States during the space race. While it didn't work very well, it's very cool to look at and snap a picture of.

While being a less often discussed invention, electric air conditioning was invented in Dayton as well. Charles Franklin Kettering, a local inventor, and philanthropist was the proud owner of the first fully air-conditioned house in the world. The invention of air conditioning is seen by some as a major turning point for America, allowing for not only more comfortable working conditions, but actually safer working conditions year round. If you're interested you can still go visit the original, still working air conditioner that was invented by Mr. Kettering by visiting his home near Kettering College of Medical Arts in Kettering Ohio.

23. GROUND TRANSPORTATION

There are only two realistic ways to get around Ohio as a visitor. Renting a car is your best option. Parking is free or inexpensive and plentiful in most places. If you plan on exploring outside of the cities, a car is a must. If you plan on sticking to the cities, or even just smaller towns, it is possible to piece together city-to-city buses. Both Greyhound and GoBus cover the area nicely. GoBus is a bus service exclusive to Ohio, connecting most Ohio towns together. Amtrak doesn't really offer intercity trains and is more of an alternative to flying to Ohio, than a way to get around.

All the large metropolitan areas in Ohio have a bus system, with Cleveland having a rail network as well. Lyft and Uber are also available in all major cities, midsize towns like Mount Vernon or Lima, and college towns. Waze Carpool is also an option.

24. OHIO'S AMISH COUNTRY

Every year more than 4 million people visit Ohio's Amish Country, just south of Wooster and north of Coshocton, and it's easy to see why. It's simple way of life is infectious and the homemade baked goods are just a bonus. With wineries, cheese houses, bakeries, quilt and craft shops, and over 80 hardwood furniture stores, be sure to leave room in your bag for the treasures you will bring home.

You have probably had Smucker's Jam before, but did you know it originated right here in Ohio? Stop by the J.M. Smucker Co. Store & Cafe where dine on homemade goodness and pick up some gift baskets for your friends. With a name like Smucker's, it has to be good! For chocolate lovers head to Coblentz Chocolates. Using fresh local butter and cream that you can purchase onsite, they create divine confections by hand in the Walnut Creek shop. Also famous in this region: cheese! Heini's Cheese Chalet is the one stop shop to get a taste of the local flavor. Offering samples on the house of over 70 different types of cheeses, you can learn about how the cheese is made and visit the fudge shop next door.

In the heart of Amish Country is Millersburg, while you're out exploring Amish country take some time to visit Historic Downtown Millersburg, which offers more than the Amish and Mennonite sites surrounding it. To get a taste of Amish life check out Schrock's Amish Farm and Village, where you can explore Amish homes, shops, and farms. Allow several hours as the village has much to offer and is worth spending time in. For a lighthearted look at Amish life visit Amish Country Theater. While it's certainly not a show the Amish themselves would see, it will entertain everyone with a family-friendly variety show.

25. BEST GARDENS IN THE STATE

While it may seem unexpected, Ohio is home to some of the best gardens in the country. The Cleveland Botanical Garden contains a highly manicured Japanese garden as well as a collection of wildflowers native to Ohio, and from all over the world. The rose garden is a highlight, and you can buy rose perfume in the gift shop. Outside of Newark, the Dawes Arboretum is free and open year round. It has a lake, forests, gardens, a Cypress Swamp with a boardwalk and various other themed gardens, as well as an impressive collection of trees from around the world. Buy a bonsai made from starters in the gift shop.

The Topiary Garden in Columbus is a seven-acre park where the art of topiary is studied, honed, and displayed. In Akron check out the Stan Hywet Hall and Gardens where you can tour the Tudor mansion as well as the rose garden, birch walk, and elegant flower beds. Cincinnati's Krohn Conservatory located in Eden Park houses a rainforest inside its walls as well as a tropical and desert house. It also has an impressive live butterfly show. In Mansfield, Kingwood Center is a center for horticultural education. The French Provincial house and surrounding gardens are open from April through October.

26. CEDAR POINT'S IMPRESSIVE COLLECTION OF 18 ROLLER COASTERS

Cedar Point has been named "Best Amusement Park in the USA" in USA TODAY, and the reasons for that are clear. The park located in Sandusky, Ohio has over 70 rides and 18 of the worlds best roller coasters. Open May through October, this 364-acre park could be enjoyed in one day but explored in many. It's perfect for the whole family, with three separate kids areas, a mile-long beach, and comfortable accommodations in the park. Longer stays warrant a trip to Cedar Point Shores Water Park next door. This 18-acre waterpark is just as fun as her dry sister and has the same great people making sure it runs just as smoothly.

27. CANTON, SMALL TOWN, BIG HEART

Canton, Ohio is a small town with all the style and benefits of a big city. Even though the population is small the community is served by The Canton Symphony Orchestra, Canton Ballet, and Canton Museum of Art, giving Canton a thriving arts scene that is already drawing attention from the art world at large. The Pro Football Hall of Fame Is probably the most famous site in Canton. Opening in 1963, it pays tribute to the brightest stars of American Football. Each year a new class of footballers is inducted into the hall of fame, drawing crowds and television audiences from across the nation. Canton is also home to the National First Ladies Library and Research Center, dedicated to researching and preserving our knowledge about America's first ladies.

America's 25th president, William McKinley, called Canton and its surrounding area home and is now entombed there at the McKinley National Monument. Open from sunrise to sunset the monument is an architectural masterpiece, and it worth exploring. Nearby in the town's center is the McKinley Presidential Library and Museum, the largest collection of McKinley artifacts in the country. Inside you will find a science museum, a discovery center, and a miniature 1800's town.

28. PUT-IN-BAY, A HISTORICAL AND RECREATION TREASURE

The pride of South Bass Island, Put-in-Bay has been used since Native American times as a place to rest or "put in at the bay" on voyages across Lake Erie. Today it hosts more tourist than weary travelers and has become a favorite vacation destination of over 1.5 million people each year. It began its journey as a tourist destination in the mid-1860s which has resulted in a Victorian Era quaintness that still clings to the island.

Today the island offers many fun activities for the vacationer, from regular island life activities like fishing and boating to Put-in-Bay exclusives like the butterfly house. Join a tour or rent a bike or golf cart, and explore the island on your own. The island has miniature golf, arcades, museums, a winery, and many historical sites. The Stonehenge Estate is considered a hidden gem on the island. A 19th estate listed on the National Register of Historic Places, Stonehenge Estate's lush green land, and historic wine press are perfect for an afternoon exploration.

While you may not expect it on an island, Put-in-Bay has two interesting caves you can explore. Perry's Cave, which houses an underground lake, was the only source of safe drinking water for the men stationed here in the battle of 1812. Lake Erie at the time was full of harmful bacteria and was making the men sick. Their recovery was instrumental in the victory of the Battle of Lake Erie. At the nearby Heineman's winery is the Crystal Cave, the world's largest geode. This cave was discovered while workers were digging a well for the winery.

The nightlife is just as exciting when the sun goes down, the lights come up. With a variety of pubs and restaurants, it's easy to find a place that caters to your needs. Whether you're looking to dance all night long, or if your in the market for something more family friendly.

29. CONTEMPLATE AT OBERLIN UNIVERSITY

A famous Ohio college town, the city of Oberlin offers a great atmosphere and a chance to relive your carefree university days. The town and College are both full of history, and today the area has its finger on the pulse of art, music, and architecture. Walking around the old town is an excursion in itself. With amazing buildings offering a look into the areas of architectural history, a highlight would be the colonnade behind Bosworth Hall with the sculpted faces of past Oberlin professors.

The college has many beautiful sculpted gardens, an area favorite would be the Japanese garden with a pond by the music conservatory.

For a more traditional look at art pop into the Oberlin Art Museum, housed in a beautiful Renaissance building. Inside you'll find a gorgeous collection of art and a seldom-used courtyard to take a break in. Inside the picturesque Finney Chapel, free music concerts take place year round. Inside there are memorials to missionaries, veterans, members of the Underground Railroad and civil rights leaders.

Back in the town, there is a wide selection of shops to visit, antique shops, used book stores, and even an old-fashioned five and dime store await near the central tree-filled square. The town has many surprises around each corner, and it's extremely easy to find them.

30. EXPLORE CENTURIES OLD EARTHWORKS

Spanning much of central Ohio are the UNESCO World Heritage sites of the Hopewell Earthworks, the highest concentration in the world, of prehistoric monumental landscape architecture. Originally one of the largest mound structures in the area the Earthworks at Newark Ohio is now half private golf course, half lazy recreation. The great circle and octagon earthworks were once connected, under what is now a midsize town. The perfectly formed, eye-level embankments align with all eight of the key rise- and set-points of the moon during its 18.6-year cycle, within a smaller margin of error than Stonehenge.

The Fort Ancient Hilltop Enclosure is over three and a half miles long and has 67 gateways, some which aline with major solar and lunar events. Mound City, near Chillicothe Ohio, is a grouping of over 25 mounds, the is the best preserved "necropolis" of the Hopewell culture. Nearby the Hopewell Culture National Historical Park has its own collection of geometric enclosures which held artifacts thought to be among the most outstanding art objects produced in pre-Columbian North America. Collectively these earthworks are an example of the height of the Woodland Period cultures of North America, offering a peek at the advanced cultures of Native Americans before colonialism.

31. SPOT A CELEB AT KENYON

Gambier, Ohio, home of the Kenyon College's hilltop campus, is surrounded by the gentle Kokosing River and the scenic rolling hills of the countryside. This beautiful college town has a surprise many people don't know about. Kenyon is the location of choice for many celebrities and politically powerful people's children. It's off the beaten track, which means little to no paparazzi. Occasionally Jamie Lee Curtis can be found in a local coffee shop or a dark corner of a restaurant. Nearby there is plenty to do, including a number of golf courses, the Kokosing Gap Trail, antiquing, canoeing and other outdoor activities.

32. THE WAYNE NATIONAL FOREST

Tucked away in the Appalachian foothills is the Wayne National Forest. The national forest exists as a patchwork across the land, enclosing more than 833,990 acres located across twelve Ohio Counties. Explore the Forest's hills, lakes, rivers, and trails where, you'll experience the natural beauty of wildflowers, rocks formations, trees, butterflies, and abundant wildlife.

Visit any time of year as every season holds its own special beauty: the white dogwoods and pink redbuds in the early spring; summertime's emerald green hills reflected in picturesque lakes; the colorful pallet of autumn; and the shiny clean beauty of a new snowfall. The wide variety of lane, from forest to plane, ensures a wide variety of wildlife habitats. Start from any entrance to discover the wild country of Ohio, with hiking both on and off the trail.

33. DISCOVER A COMPREHENSIVE COLLECTION OF CONTRACEPTIVES

An impressive collection of over one thousand items, Cleveland's Percy Skuy Collection on the History of Contraception is like no museum you've ever been to. With items ranging from beaver testicles to rhythm beads to IUDs, it shows the great lengths that humans will go inspired by that ageless muse known as sex. Throughout history, humans have gone to great lengths in order to avoid pregnancies while not having to refrain from sex. Here you can find first-hand accounts of these measures in the past, such as notes from the journals of Casanova and ancient texts, dating to 1580 BCE. Originally conceived by Canadian pharmacy executive Percy Skuy as a private educational museum, the universally appealing subject matter quickly propelled the museum into the public domain.

34. EXPLORE THE CINCINNATI FOOD SCENE

With local cuisines different than that of the rest of Ohio, "Cincy" is worth exploring for its food culture alone. Cincinnati-Style Chili is so unique that it can be hard to find even in other areas of Ohio. This recipe developed by Macedonian immigrant restaurateurs in the 1920s contains a Mediterranean-spiced meat sauce and is used as a topping for spaghetti called a "two-way" or hot dogs called "coneys."With over 150 specialty chili restaurants in Cincinnati alone, the residents of the area eat over 2 million pounds of chili each year. Though not a part of the south, Cincinnati has its own barbecue recipe to rival that of Memphis or Dallas, the Montgomery Inn Barbeque Sauce. To eat meat like a local head to one of the three locations across the area or buy some of the sauce to take home for yourself. Cincinnati, like much of Ohio, was the home to many resettled Germans, who left their mark on the culinary scene as well. Goetta, a dish often referred to as "Cincinnati Caviar", is an area favorite. Made mostly of ground meat and steel-cut oats with seasonings, the dish is only found in Cincinnati and is produced in masse by Glier's Goetta.

35. ASHTABULA COUNTY COVERED BRIDGES

Ashtabula County, the "Covered Bridge Capital of Ohio," has had 62 covered bridges over its rivers at one time or another. Today there remain 19 covered bridges in Ashtabula County, including the longest and the shortest ones in the entire United States. The longest measuring in at 613 feet with The Shortest Functioning Covered Bridge in the United State record holder consisting of only 18 feet of wood and nails.

Most of these majestic wooden masterpieces date as far back as the 1850's, while others are more modern, with seven of the bridges built after 1984. All considered to be marvels of engineering and all are reminiscent of the time and style of a bygone era. They span some of the most beautiful, scenic, river valleys in the region. Pick up a guidebook of the area from any of the rangers stations and head out to find all 19 of this gorgeous bridges.

36. HOCKING HILLS STATE PARK

Located in southeastern Ohio Hocking Hills State Park is the crown jewel of Hocking county. The beautiful park and forest stretching for 2,356 acres have amazing waterfalls and caves you can explore towering cliffs, waterfalls and deep, hemlock-shaded gorges for hikers. Whether you want to go on a short walk or multi-day hike this is a great place to visit. A favorite is Rock House a large cave where Native Americans lived. Still visible on the ceiling and walls are drawings and smoke stains from when it was inhabited by the Native Americans who used it for shelter in the winter and a cool place in the summer. The most popular attraction is Old Man's Cave, which earned its moniker from the hermit Richard Rowe who lived in the large caves of the gorge.

37. ROCK OUT AT CLEVELAND'S ROCK AND ROLL HALL OF FAME

In the mid-1980s the Rock & Roll Hall of Fame Foundation was looking for a place to call home. Many iconic cities like New York, San Francisco, and Chicago all made bids. Due to a groundswell of public support and a $65 million commitment from the city, Cleveland became the site of the Rock and Roll Hall of Fame Museum. It opened in 1995 to much fanfare with many well-known musicians, such as The Who and Billy Joel, in attendance. Today it's a great place to see every bit of rock and roll music history right down to the dress Janis Joplin wore to Woodstock

38. VELVET ICE CREAM FACTORY

Joseph Dager was only 15 when he first landed in America in 1903. Unable to speak English, he started out to search for the American dream. Eleven years later, in the basement of a small confectionery in Utica, Ohio, Dager would achieve that dream. There he sold his first batch of homemade, hand-cranked vanilla ice cream and Velvet Ice Cream was born.

Ye Old Mill, just outside of Utica is now home to an ice cream factory, with a yearly festival and season ground full of trees, lakes, and animals. Take the free 30-minute walking tour, and get a glimpse into the history of the mill and Velvet ice cream, before heading to the Viewing Gallery to see how the ice cream gets made first hand. Each summer more than 150,000 come to Utica to taste fresh ice cream and explore the 20 picturesque acres of rolling hills and thick forests.

39. LEARN IN THE HIDDEN MUSEUMS OF UNION TERMINAL

The mosaic-filled, striking Union Terminal is an Art Deco masterpiece from 1933. Inside one of the last great train stations built here in America, you'll find several museums dedicated to history and science as well as a children's museum. Feast your eyes on the intricate details and stories of the Winold Reiss mosaics, visit Tower A (the original control tower) or purchase a sweet treat in the Rookwood-tiled ice cream parlor, which hasn't changed since it first opened.

Keep an eye open for the interpreters in costumes helping locals and visitors to find a connection to the past in the history museum. Kids will want to explore the areas made just for them such as the Energy Zone, Little Sprouts Farm and Kid's Town at Duke Energy Children's Museum. Take a peek into the Last Great Ice Age, and go back in time over 19,000 years in Museum of Natural History and Science.

40. AMERICAN SIGN MUSEUM

The American Sign Museum was created by Tod Swormstedt, and opened in 2005. The grandson of H. C. Menefee, the first editor of Sign of the Times, the sign industry's main periodical, it would seem signs are the family business. The museum is dedicated to the art and history of signs and sign making. The Museum's collection starts in the 1800s and continues on until around the 1970s. The collection spans from pristine still-in-the-box signs to ones that have far outlived their intended use. With over 500 signs the collection's highlights include Sputnik-like "Satellite" sign, hand-built to advertise a strip mall, a single-arch McDonald's sign with the pre-Ronald "Speedee" character and a full-size, Mail Pouch sign from the side of a barn, reassembled in a room with other local signs.

41. EARLY TELEVISION MUSEUM

Just 20 minutes from downtown Columbus sits Steve McVoy hobby turned public works project, the Early Television Museum. McVoy always loved television, working as a repairman and then running a cable TV business. In 1999 he retired and began collecting vintage television sets. Before too long his collection got so out of hand he had to move it to its own building, now the Early Television Museum.

The museum contains over 200 Vs from 1928 through 1962. There are mechanical sets from the 1920s and '30s, pre-war British and American televisions from the late '30s and early '40s, post-war TVs from 1945 to 1958, and early color ones from the 1950s. Most of the sets still work and are set up so the era-appropriate material can be viewed on them by pressing a button.

42. EXPLORE A CZAR FUNDED CHURCH IN CLEVELAND

One of the most spectacular churches in America, this textbook examples of Russian architecture is unlike anything else in Ohio. The Saint Theodosius Orthodox Cathedral was built in the early years of the 20th century and was funded in part by Czar Nicholas II's missionary fund. With a lavish onion-domed and enough murals to keep even the most sleep-deprived parishioners engaged.

Designed by Cleveland architect Frederick Baird, the church wouldn't receive its distinctive murals until after 1950. The murals, painted by Andrej Bicenko cover every bit of wall space with Christ and his saints, in rich tones of red, blue, and gold. Over the years smoke from the candles and nearby steel mills would damage the murals, which were restored around the turn of the century.

In portrait on the iconostasis is Herman of Alaska, the patron saint of Orthodox Christians in America. He was a famed Russian missionary who settled in Alaska in 1794 and would receive sainthood in 1969. Recognize the place? That's because it was used in the 1978 movie The Deer Hunter for a wedding scene. Michael Cimino even cast St. Theodosius's actual priest as the officiating priest.

43. ADMIRE 1,000-YEAR-OLD ROCK CARVINGS FROM A MYSTERIOUS VANISHED NORTH AMERICAN CULTURE.

Outside of Ray, Ohio, you'll find some of the best-preserved rock art in Ohio. The nearly 40 figures, collectively known as the Leo Petroglyph, form an eclectic blend of straightforward designs and abstract images, preserving traces of a vanished Native American culture. Thought to be made by the Fort Ancient culture people, scientists think that these ancient people began carving the mysterious petroglyphs into the flat sandstone canvas about 1,000 years ago.

Originally found over the gorge in a sandstone hillside, the petroglyph was moved to its current position under a shelter to help preserve it from the elements. Hope for a bit of rain to scare away the other tourist so you get the whole place to yourself. You'll also be able to see how the water drains over the rock overhangs and down into the small gorge.

The short nature trail is worth checking out, it winds into the gorge around bedrock overhangs possibly used by ancient natives as shelter, and back up to the parking area.

44. FAMOUS GRAVESITES

A lot of famous people are from Ohio, and as a result, many are buried here. Below is a list of the graves of the most prominent people in Ohio. (Graves discussed elsewhere not listed)

Rutherford B.Hayes – The 19th President of the United States (Fremont, Ohio)

Annie Oakley – The famous woman sharpshooter (Brock Cemetery outside of Greenville, Ohio)

Moses Fleetwood "Fleet" Walker – The first black player in MLB (Union Cemetery in Steubenville, Ohio)

John Davison Rockefeller, Sr - Businessman and Philanthropist (Lake View Cemetery, Cleveland, Ohio.)

James Garfield - 20th President of the United States (Lake View Cemetery, Cleveland, Ohio.)

Eddie Rickenbacker - Fighter Pilot, 'Ace of Aces' during World War I. (Greenlawn Cemetery, Columbus, Ohio)

Paul Lynde - Queer Actor and Comedian (Amity Cemetery Knox County, Ohio)

Balto the Wonder Dog - Life-Saving Hero Sled-Dog (Cleveland Museum of Natural History)

Eliot Ness - Prohibition agent, famous for his efforts to enforce Prohibition in Chicago, Illinois and bringing down Al Capone. (Lake View Cemetery, Cleveland, Ohio.)

William Henry Harrison - 9th President of the United States (North Bend, Ohio)

Woody Hayes - Famous College Football Coach (Union Cemetery, Columbus, Ohio)

Orville and Wilbur Wright – Fathers of aviation and inventors of the airplane. (Woodland Cemetery in Dayton, Ohio)

Aunt Jemima (Rosie Riles) – The pancake queen. (Redoak, Ohio)

Kent State Memorial – Memorial dedicated to four university students who were killed by the National Guard on May 4, 1970, during a protest. The markers are placed where each of the four died as a reminder to always fight back.

45. LIVE MUSIC SCENE

Columbus' Arena District host live music every weekend, during the summer look for the LIVE concert series with free performances in local parks. The new downtown area is thriving with new restaurants and bars hosting local musicians for lively evening performances on weeknights and weekends. Nationwide Arena brings the big-name artist from around the world every weekend for exciting concerts. In Cleveland the Rock and Roll hall of fame both showcases pieces of rock and roll history and is also a venue for live music, hosting many up and coming stars. If you love music this is a place you should dedicate a day and perhaps an evening to. For more live music check out Cleveland's House of Blues or Euclid's Grogg Shop. In the summer, Cincinnati's Fountain Square becomes an outdoor gathering point for locals and visitors, hosting live music act5s and other entertainment all summer long.

46. DRIVE ACROSS A FAVORITE BRIDGE OF AMELIA EARHART

The Y-Bridge of Zanesville, Ohio is literally one-of-a-kind, is built at the confluence of the Licking and Muskingum Rivers. The fast rushing water and multiple rivers merging made for difficulty when it came to getting across said waters. In 1814, engineers determined that a unique, y-shaped bridge was the answer to their problem. The design was so unique that pioneering aviator Amelia Earhart once remarked that it made Zanesville "the most recognizable city in the country." The current bridge, with an intersection in the middle of the water, is the 5th to have stood in the same spot, all of them Y-shaped. As time passes, and no better solution is devised, it's clear to see that the problem is already more than solved. Regardless the Y-City Bridge remains one of the few bridges in the world that can be crossed without changing sides of the river.

47. VISIT CLEVELAND'S MOST HAUNTED HOUSE

Franklin Castle, often referred to as "The Most Haunted House in Ohio," was built in the 1880s by grocer-turned-banker Hannes Tiedemann. Even his fortune couldn't keep him from a tragic life. Many of his family died inside the walls elaborately turreted walls, including his 15-year-old daughter, his mother, and three additional children, who died in infancy. It is said that the constant construction on the property was a distraction for Mrs. Tiedemann, who would eventually succumb to what locals were now calling "the curse."

The house found a new life, after Tiedemann sold, as a German cultural center. It wasn't until the mid-1960s that rumors of hauntings in the form of surging electricity, the sound of babies crying, and a mysterious woman in black started pouring out of the house. In 1975 human bones were found in a closet, and soon after the new owners began offering ghost tours.

The house changed hands several times and was eventually left abandoned, in 2011 Franklin Castle was purchased by the current owners and is now closed off from the public. To get a good view of this purportedly haunted site, look for the crowd on the sidewalk on Franklin Boulevard.

48. TAKE A TRIP BACK IN TIME ON THE ERIE CANAL

Get transported back to the 1830's at Coshocton's Roscoe Village. Here you can experience what it was like when the Ohio and Erie Canal was bustling with Canal boats. The restored Canal town is a full working village fill with costumed actors playing the roles of its residents. Follow in the footsteps of living history, take a walk through the meticulous gardens, tour the museums and living exhibits and experience what horse-drawn canal boat ride on a section of the Erie Canal was like almost two centuries ago.

49. CELEBRATE THE HEROINES OF AVIATION HISTORY

The International Women's Air & Space Museum is located inside Burke Lakefront Airport terminal, The space blends seamlessly into the airport, and sporadically placed glass cases enclose memorabilia like the helmet worn by Ruby Wine Sheldon and the vintage uniform of the first airline stewardesses. Every couple of feet you can find documents, replicas, photographs, and model planes. The museum showcases the achievements of some of America's women, the bravest and most daring of their time. Nested away in the "Birthplace of Aviation," this museum is a tribute to how hard these women had to work to get even half the recognition of their male peers.

50. MALABAR FARM STATE PARK

Malabar Farm in Pleasant Valley was the passion of the Pulitzer Prize-winning author, Louis Bromfield. Today little has changed, the house and farm stand just as they did in Bromfield's time. The surrounding buildings and land housing chickens, goats and beef cattle while the fields boast corn, wheat, oats, and hay. Scenic trails crisscross the area, showcasing the natural bounty of the land.

Malabar Fame's has also found fame as a golden age of Hollywood hotspot. Humphrey Bogart, Lauren Bacall, James Cagney, and other Hollywood types partied in the house set on the rolling hills of north central Ohio. Today visit the 32-room Big House, designed by Bromfield. Sign up for house tours and wagon rides, or even educational tours of its vegetable garden.

BONUS BOOK

50 THINGS TO KNOW ABOUT PACKING LIGHT FOR TRAVEL

PACK THE RIGHT WAY EVERY TIME

AUTHOR: MANIDIPA BHATTACHARYYA

Edited by Melanie Howthorne

ABOUT THE AUTHOR

Manidipa Bhattacharyya is a creative writer and editor, with an education in English literature and Linguistics. After working in the IT industry for seven long years she decided to call it quits and follow her heart instead. Manidipa has been ghost writing, editing, proof reading and doing secondary research services for many story tellers and article writers for about three years. She stays in Kolkata, India with her husband and a busy two year old. In her own time Manidipa enjoys travelling, photography and writing flash fiction.

Manidipa believes in travelling light and never carries anything that she couldn't haul herself on a trip. However, travelling with her child changed the scenario. She seemed to carry the entire world with her for the baby on the first two trips. But good sense prevailed and she is again working her way to becoming a light traveler, this time with a kid.

INTRODUCTION

*He who would travel happily
must travel light.*

-Antoine de Saint-Exupéry

Travel takes you to different places from seas and mountains to deserts and much more. In your travels you get to interact with different people and their cultures. You will, however, enjoy the sights and interact positively with these new people even more, if you are travelling light.

When you travel light your mind can be free from worry about your belongings. You do not have to spend precious vacation time waiting for your luggage to arrive after a long flight. There is be no chance of your bags going missing and the best part is that you need not pay a fee for checked baggage.

People who have mastered this art of packing light will root for you to take only one carry-on, wherever you go. However, many people can find it really hard to pack light. More so if you are travelling with children. Differentiating between "must have" and "just in case" items is the starting point. There will be ample shopping avenues at your destination which are just waiting to be explored.

This book will show you 'packing' in a new 'light' –
pun intended – and help you to embrace light
packing practices for all of your future travels.

Off to packing!

DEDICATION

I dedicate this book to all the travel buffs that I know,
who have given me great insights into the contents of
their backpacks.

THE RIGHT TRAVEL GEAR

1. CHOOSE YOUR TRAVEL GEAR CAREFULLY

While selecting your travel gear, pick items that are
light weight, durable and most importantly, easy to
carry. There are cases with wheels so you can drag
them along – these are usually on the heavy side
because of the trolley. Alternatively a backpack that
you can carry comfortably on your back, or even a
duffel bag that you can carry easily by hand or sling
across your body are also great options. Whatever
you choose, one thing to keep in mind is that the
luggage itself should not weigh a ton, this will give
you the flexibility to bring along one extra pair of
shoes if you so desire.

2. CARRY THE MINIMUM NUMBER OF BAGS

Selecting light weight luggage is not everything. You need to restrict the number of bags you carry as well. One carry-on size bag is ideal for light travel. Most carriers allow one cabin baggage plus one purse, handbag or camera bag as long as it slides under the seat in front. So technically, you can carry two items of luggage without checking them in.

3. PACK ONE EXTRA BAG

Always pack one extra empty bag along with your essential items. This could be a very light weight duffel bag or even a sturdy tote bag which takes up minimal space. In the event that you end up buying a lot of souvenirs, you already have a handy bag to stuff all that into and do not have to spend time hunting for an appropriate bag.

I'm very strict with my packing and have everything in its right place. I never change a rule. I hardly use anything in the hotel room. I wheel my own wardrobe in and that's it.

Charlie Watts

CLOTHES & ACCESSORIES

4. PLAN AHEAD

Figure out in advance what you plan to do on your trip. That will help you to pick that one dress you need for the occasion. If you are going to attend a wedding then you have to carry formal wear. If not, you can ditch the gown for something lighter that will be comfortable during long walks or on the beach.

5. WEAR THAT JACKET

Remember that wearing items will not add extra luggage for your air travel. So wear that bulky jacket that you plan to carry for your trip. This saves space and can also help keep you warm during the chilly flight.

6. MIX AND MATCH

Carry clothes that can be interchangeably used to reinvent your look. Find one top that goes well with a couple of pairs of pants or skirts. Use tops, shirts and jackets wisely along with other accessories like a scarf or a stole to create a new look.

7. CHOOSE YOUR FABRIC WISELY

Stuffing clothes in cramped bags definitely takes its toll which results in wrinkles. It is best to carry wrinkle free, synthetic clothes or merino tops. This will eliminate the need for that small iron you usually bring along.

8. DITCH CLOTHES PACK UNDERWEAR

Pack more underwear and socks. These are the things that will give you a fresh feel even if you do not get a chance to wear fresh clothes. Moreover these are easy to wash and can be dried inside the hotel room itself.

9. CHOOSE DARK OVER LIGHT

While picking your clothes choose dark coloured ones. They are easy to colour coordinate and can last longer before needing a wash. Accidental food spills and dirt from the road are less visible on darker clothes.

10. WEAR YOUR JEANS

Take only one pair of Jeans with you, which you should wear on the flight. Remember to pick a pair that can be worn for sightseeing trips and is equally eloquent for dinner. You can add variety by adding light weight cargoes and chinos.

11. CARRY SMART ACCESSORIES

The right accessory can give you a fresh look even with the same old dress. An intelligent neck-piece, a couple of bright scarves, stoles or a sarong can be used in a number of ways to add variety to your clothing. These light weight beauties can double up as a nursing cover, a light blanket, beach wear, a modesty cover for visiting places of worship, and also makes for an enthralling game of peek-a-boo.

12. LEARN TO FOLD YOUR GARMENTS

Seasoned travellers all swear by rolling their clothes for compact and wrinkle free packing. Bundle packing, where you roll the clothes around a central object as if tying it up, is also a popular method of compact and wrinkle free packing. Stacking folded clothes one on top of another is a big no-no as it makes creases extreme and they are difficult to get rid of without ironing.

13. WASH YOUR DIRTY LAUNDRY

One of the ways to avoid carrying loads of clothes is to wash the clothes you carry. At some places you might get to use the laundry services or a Laundromat but if you are in a pinch, best solution is to wash them yourself. If that is the plan then carrying quick drying clothes is highly recommended, which most often also happen to be the wrinkle free variety.

14. LEAVE THOSE TOWELS BEHIND

Regular towels take up a lot of space, are heavy and take ages to dry out. If you are staying at hotels they will provide you with towels anyway. If you are travelling to a remote place, where the availability of towels look doubtful, carry a light weight travel towel of viscose material to do the job.

15. USE A COMPRESSION BAG

Compression bags are getting lots of recommendation now days from regular travellers. These are useful for saving space in your luggage when you have to pack bulky dresses. While packing for the return trip, get help from the hotel staff to arrange a vacuum cleaner.

FOOTWEAR

16. PUT ON YOUR HIKING BOOTS

If you have plans to go hiking or trekking during your trip, you will need those bulky hiking boots. The best way to carry them is to wear them on flight to save space and luggage weight. You can remove the boots once inside and be comfortable in your socks.

17. PICKING THE RIGHT SHOES

Shoes are often the bulkiest items, along with being the dainty if you are a female. They need care and take up a lot of space in your luggage. It is advisable therefore to pick shoes very carefully. If you plan to do a lot of walking and site seeing, then wearing a pair of comfortable walking shoes are a must. For more formal occasions you can carry durable, light weight flats which will not take up much space.

18. STUFF SHOES

If you happen to pack a pair of shoes, ensure you utilize their hollow insides. Tuck small items like rolled up socks or belts to save space. They will also be easy to find.

TOILETRIES

19. STASHING TOILETRIES

Carry only absolute necessities. Airline rules dictate
that for one carry-on bag, liquids and gels must be in
3.4 ounce (100ml) bottles or less, and must be packed
in a one quart zip-lock bag. If you are planning to stay
in a hotel, the basic things will be provided for you.
It's best is to buy the rest from the local market at
your destination.

20. TAKE ALONG TAMPONS

Tampons are a hard to find item in a lot of countries.
Figure out how many you need and pack accordingly.
For longer stays you can buy them online and have
them delivered to where you are staying.

21. GET PAMPERED BEFORE YOU TRAVEL

Some avid travellers suggest getting a pedicure and
manicure just the day before travelling. This not only
gives you a well kept look, you also save the trouble
of packing nail polish. Remember, every little bit of
weight reduced adds up.

ELECTRONICS

22. LUGGING ALONG ELECTRONICS

Electronics have a large role to play in our lives today. Most of us cannot imagine our lives away from our phones, laptops or tablets. However while travelling, one must consider the amount of weight these electronics add to our luggage. Thankfully smart phones come along with all the essentials tools like a camera, email access, picture editing tools and more. They are smart to the point of eliminating the need to carry multiple gadgets. Choose a smart phone that suits all your requirements and travel with the world in your palms or pocket.

23. REDUCE THE NUMBER OF CHARGERS

If you do travel with multiple electronic devices, you will have to bear the additional burden of carrying all their chargers too. Check if a single charger can be used for multiple devices. You might also consider investing in a pocket charger. These small devices support multiple devices while keeping you charged on the go.

24. TRAVEL FRIENDLY APPS

Along with smart phones come numerous apps, which are immensely helpful in our travels. You name it and you have an app for it at hand – take pictures, sharing with friends and family, torch to light dark roads, maps, checking flight/train times, find hotels and many other things. Use these smart alternatives to traditional items like books to eliminate weight and save space.

I get ideas about what's essential when packing my suitcase.

-Diane von Furstenberg

TRAVELLING WITH KIDS

25. BRING ALONG THE STROLLER

Kids might enjoy walking for a while but they soon tire out and a stroller is the just the right thing for them to rest in while you continue your tour. Strollers also double duty as a luggage carrier and shopping bag holder. Remember to pick a light weight, easy to handle brand of stroller. Better yet, find out in advance if you can rent a stroller at your destination.

26. BRING ONLY ENOUGH DIAPERS FOR YOUR TRIP

Diapers take up a lot of space and add to the weight of your luggage. Therefore it is advisable to carry just enough diapers to last through the trip and a few for afterwards, till you buy fresh stock at your destination. Unless of course you are travelling to a really remote area, in which case you have no choice but to carry the load. Otherwise diapers are something you will find pretty easily.

27. TAKE ONLY A COUPLE OF TOYS

Children are easily attracted by new things in their environment. While travelling they will find numerous 'new' objects to scrutinize and play with. Packing just one favorite toy is enough, or if there is no favorite toy leave out all of them in favor of stories or imaginary games.

28. CARRY KID FRIENDLY SNACKS

Create a small snack counter in your bag to store away quick bites for those sudden hunger pangs. Depending on the child's age this could include chocolates, raisins, dry fruits, granola bars or biscuits. Also keep a bottle of water handy for your little one.

These things do not add much weight and can be adjusted in a handbag or knapsack.

29. GAMES TO CARRY

Create some travel specific, imaginary games if you have slightly grown up children, like spot the attractions. Keep a coloring book and colors handy for in-flight or hotel time. Apps on your smart phone can keep the children engaged with cartoons and story books. Older children are often entertained by games available on phones or tablets. This cuts the weight of luggage down while keeping the kids entertained.

30. LET THE KIDS CARRY THEIR LOAD

A good thing is to start early sharing of responsibilities. Let your child pick a bag of his or her choice and pack it themselves. Keep tabs on what they are stuffing in their bags by asking if they will be using that item on the trip. It could start out being just an entertainment bag initially but with growing years they will learn to sort the useful from the superfluous. Children as little as four can maneuver a small trolley suitcase like a pro- their experience in pull along toys credit. If you are worried that you may be pulling it for them, you may want to start with a backpack.

31. DECIDE ON LOCATION FOR CHILDREN TO SLEEP

While on a trip you might not always get a crib at your destination, and carrying one will make life all the more difficult. Instead call ahead to see if there are any cribs or roll out beds for children. You may even put blankets on the floor. Weave them a story about camping and they will gladly sleep without any trouble.

32. GET BABY PRODUCTS DELIVERED AT YOUR DESTINATION

If you are absolutely paranoid about not getting your favourite variety of diaper or brand of baby food, check out online stores like amazon.com for services in your destination city. You can buy things online ahead of your travel and get them delivered to your hotel upon arrival.

33. FEEDING NEEDS OF YOUR INFANTS

If you are travelling with a breastfed infant, you save the trouble of carrying bottles and bottle sanitization kits. For special food, or medications, you may need to call ahead to make sure you have a refrigerator where you are staying.

34. FEEDING NEEDS OF YOUR TODDLER

With the progression from infancy to toddler, their dietary requirements too evolve. You will have to pack some snacks for travelling time. Fresh fruits and vegetables can be purchased at your destination. Most of the cities you travel to in whichever part of the world, will have baby food products and formulas, available at the local drug-store or the supermarket.

35. PICKING CLOTHES FOR YOUR BABY

Contrary to popular belief, babies can do without many changes of clothes. At the most pack 2 outfits per day. Pack mix and match type clothes for your little one as well. Pick things which are comfortable to wear and quick to dry.

36. SELECTING SHOES FOR YOUR BABY

Like outfits, kids can make do with two pairs of comfortable shoes. If you can get some water resistant shoes it will be best. To expedite drying wet shoes, you can stuff newspaper in them then wrap them with newspaper and leave them to dry overnight.

37. KEEP ONE CHANGE OF CLOTHES HANDY

Travelling with kids can be tricky. Keep a change of clothes for the kids and mum handy in your purse or tote bag. This takes a bit of space in your hand luggage but comes extremely handy in case there are any accidents or spills.

38. LEAVE BEHIND BABY ACCESSORIES

Baby accessories like their bed, bath tub, car seat, crib etc. should be left at home. Many hotels provide a crib on request, while car seats can be borrowed from friends or rented. Babies can be given a bath in the hotel sink or even in the adult bath tub with a little bit of water. If you bring a few bath toys, they can be used in the bath, pool, and out of water. They can also be sanitized easily in the sink.

39. CARRY A SMALL LOAD OF PLASTIC BAGS

With children around there are chances of a number of soiled clothes and diapers. These plastic bags help to sort the dirt from the clean inside your big bag.

These are very light weight and come in handy to other carry stuff as well at times.

PACK WITH A PURPOSE

40. PACKING FOR BUSINESS TRIPS

One neutral-colored suit should suffice. It can be paired with different shirts, ties and accessories for different occasions. One pair of black suit pants could be worn with a matching jacket for the office or with a snazzy top for dinner.

41. PACKING FOR A CRUISE

Most cruises have formal dinners, and that formal dress usually takes up a lot of space. However you might find a tuxedo to rent. For women, a short black dress with multiple accessory options will do the trick.

42. PACKING FOR A LONG TRIP OVER DIFFERENT CLIMATES

The secret packing mantra for travel over multiple climates is layering. Layering traps air around your body creating insulation against the cold. The same light t-shirt that is comfortable in a warmer climate can be the innermost layer in a colder climate.

REDUCE SOME MORE WEIGHT

43. LEAVE PRECIOUS THINGS AT HOME

Things that you would hate to lose or get damaged leave them at home. Precious jewelry, expensive gadgets or dresses, could be anything. You will not require these on your trip. Leave them at home and spare the load on your mind.

44. SEND SOUVENIRS BY MAIL

If you have spent all your money on purchasing souvenirs, carrying them back in the same bag that you brought along would be difficult. Either pack everything in another bag and check it in the airport or get everything shipped to your home. Use an international carrier for a secure transit, but this could be more expensive than the checking fees at the airport.

45. AVOID CARRYING BOOKS

Books equal to weight. There are many reading apps which you can download on your smart phone or tab.

Plus there are gadgets like Kindle and Nook that are thinner and lighter alternatives to your regular book.

CHECK, GET, SET, CHECK AGAIN

46. STRATEGIZE BEFORE PACKING

Create a travel list and prepare all that you think you need to carry along. Keep everything on your bed or floor before packing and then think through once again – do I really need that? Any item that meets this question can be avoided. Remove whatever you don't really need and pack the rest.

47. TEST YOUR LUGGAGE

Once you have fully packed for the trip take a test trip with your luggage. Take your bags and go to town for window shopping for an hour. If you enjoy your hour long trip it is good to go, if not, go home and reduce the load some more. Repeat this test till you hit the right weight.

48. ADD A ROLL OF DUCT TAPE

You might wonder why, when this book has been talking about reducing stuff, we're suddenly asking you to pack something totally unusual. This is because when you have limited supplies, duct tape is immensely helpful for small repairs – a broken bag, leaking zip-lock bag, broken sunglasses, you name it and duct tape can fix it, temporarily.

49. LIST OF ESSENTIAL ITEMS

Even though the emphasis is on packing light, there are things which have to be carried for any trip. Here is our list of essentials:

• Passport/Visa or any other ID

• Any other paper work that might be required on a trip like permits, hotel reservation confirmations etc.

• Medicines – all your prescription medicines and emergency kit, especially if you are travelling with children

• Medical or vaccination records

• Money in foreign currency if travelling to a different country

• Tickets- Email or Message them to your phone

50. MAKE THE MOST OF YOUR TRIP

Wherever you are going, whatever you hope to do we encourage you to embrace it whole-heartedly. Take in the scenery, the culture and above all, enjoy your time away from home.

On a long journey even a straw weighs heavy.

-Spanish Proverb

PACKING AND PLANNING TIPS

A Week before Leaving

- Arrange for someone to take care of pets and water plants.

- Stop mail and newspaper.

- Notify Credit Card companies where you are going.

- Change your thermostat settings.

- Car inspected, oil is changed, and tires have the correct pressure.

- Passports and photo identification is up to date.

- Pay bills.

- Copy important items and download travel Apps.

- Start collecting small bills for tips.

Right Before Leaving

- Clean out refrigerator.

- Empty garbage cans.

- Lock windows.

- Make sure you have the proper identification with you.

- Bring cash for tips.

- Remember travel documents.

- Lock door behind you.

- Remember wallet.

- Unplug items in house and pack chargers.

READ OTHER
GREATER THAN A TOURIST
BOOKS

> TOURIST

Visit Greater Than a Tourist for Free Travel Tips
http://GreaterThanATourist.com

Sign up for the Greater Than a Tourist Newsletter for discount days, new books, and travel information:
http://eepurl.com/cxspyf

Follow us on Facebook for tips, images, and ideas:
https://www.facebook.com/GreaterThanATourist

Follow us on Pinterest for travel tips and ideas:
http://pinterest.com/GreaterThanATourist

Follow us on Instagram for beautiful travel images:
http://Instagram.com/GreaterThanATourist

> TOURIST

Please leave your honest review of this book on Amazon and Goodreads. Please send your feedback to GreaterThanaTourist@gmail.com as we continue to improve the series. We appreciate your positive and constructive feedback. Thank you.

METRIC CONVERSIONS

TEMPERATURE

110° F — — 40° C
100° F —
90° F — — 30° C
80° F —
70° F — — 20° C
60° F —
50° F — — 10° C
40° F —
32° F — — 0° C
20° F —
10° F — — -10° C
0° F —
-10° F — — -18° C
-20° F — — -30° C

To convert F to C:

Subtract 32, and then multiply by 5/9 or .5555.

To Convert C to F:

Multiply by 1.8 and then add 32.

32F = 0C

LIQUID VOLUME

To Convert:...................Multiply by
U.S. Gallons to Liters................ 3.8
U.S. Liters to Gallons 26
Imperial Gallons to U.S. Gallons 1.2
Imperial Gallons to Liters....... 4.55
Liters to Imperial Gallons 22
1 Liter = .26 U.S. Gallon
1 U.S. Gallon = 3.8 Liters

DISTANCE

To convert ....Multiply by
Inches to Centimeters 2.54
Centimeters to Inches 39
Feet to Meters....................... .3
Meters to Feet 3.28
Yards to Meters 91
Meters to Yards 1.09
Miles to Kilometers 1.61
Kilometers to Miles............ .62
1 Mile = 1.6 km
1 km = .62 Miles

WEIGHT

1 Ounce = .28 Grams
1 Pound = .4555 Kilograms
1 Gram = .04 Ounce
1 Kilogram = 2.2 Pounds

TRAVEL QUESTIONS

- Do you bring presents home to family or friends after a vacation?

- Do you get motion sick?

- Do you have a favorite billboard?

- Do you know what to do if there is a flat tire?

- Do you like a sun roof open?

- Do you like to eat in the car?

- Do you like to wear sun glasses in the car?

- Do you like toppings on your ice cream?

- Do you use public bathrooms?

- Did you bring your cell phone and does it have power?

- Do you have a form of identification with you?

- Have you ever been pulled over by a cop?

- Have you ever given money to a stranger on a road trip?

- Have you ever taken a road trip with animals?

- Have you ever went on a vacation alone?

- Have you ever run out of gas?

- If you could move to any place in the world, where would it be?

- If you could travel anywhere in the world, where would you travel?

- If you could travel in any vehicle, which one would it be?

- If you had three things to wish for from a magic genie, what would they be?

- If you have a driver's license, how many times did it take you to pass the test?

- What are you the most afraid of on vacation?

- What do you want to get away from the most when you are on vacation?

- What foods smells bad to you?

- What item do you bring on ever trip with you away from home?

- What makes you sleepy?

- What song would you love to hear on the radio when you're cruising on the highway?

- What travel job would you want the least?

- What will you miss most while you are away from home?

- What is something you always wanted to try?

- What is the best road side attraction that you ever saw?

- What is the farthest distance you ever biked?

- What is the farthest distance you ever walked?

- What is the weirdest thing you needed to buy while on vacation?

- What is your favorite candy?

- What is your favorite color car?

- What is your favorite family vacation?

- What is your favorite food?

- What is your favorite gas station drink or food?

- What is your favorite license plate design?

- What is your favorite restaurant?

- What is your favorite smell?

- What is your favorite song?

- What is your favorite sound that nature makes?

- What is your favorite thing to bring home from a vacation?

- What is your favorite vacation with friends?

- What is your favorite way to relax?

- Where is the farthest place you ever traveled in a car?

- Where is the farthest place you ever went North, South, East and West?

- Where is your favorite place in the world?

- Who is your favorite singer?

- Who taught you how to drive?

- Who will you miss the most while you are away?

- Who if the first person you will contact when you get to your destination?

- Who brought you on your first vacation?

- Who likes to travel the most in your life?

- Would you rather be hot or cold?

- Would you rather drive above, below, or at the speed limited?

- Would you rather drive on a highway or a back road?

- Would you rather go on a train or a boat?

- Would you rather go to the beach or the woods?

TRAVEL BUCKET LIST

1.

2.

3.

4.

5.

6.

7.

8.

9.

10.

NOTES

Made in the USA
Monee, IL
19 April 2022